THE NEW PHYSICS

The Wesleyan Poetry Program : Volume 97

THE NEW

POEMS BY

Middletown, Connecticut

PHYSICS.

AL ZOLYNAS

Wesleyan University Press

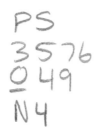

Grateful acknowledgement is made to the following publications, in which some of these poems have appeared: *An Adult Coloring Book* (anthology); *Aspen Leaves; Crazy Horse; Dacotah Territory; Eating the Menu: A Contemporary American Poetry, 1970–74; The Great Oasis; The Kansas City Star; A Lake Superior Journal; Loon; The Minneapolis Tribune; Minnesota Poetry Outloud Anthology, 1976; Moons and Lion Tailes; Poet and Critic; Poetry Australia; The Small Farm; Specialia, A Contemporary American Poetry; Steelhead; Western Review.*

Library of Congress Cataloging in Publication Data

Zolynas, Al, 1945–
    The new physics.

    (Wesleyan poetry program; 97)
    I. Title.
PS3576.049N4   811'.5'4   79–65337
ISBN 0–8195–2097–7
ISBN 0–8195–1097–1 pbk.

Manufactured in the United States of America
First edition

To Arlie, my wife, and Kostas and Ona, my parents

CONTENTS

III. STRANGENESS

I. COLOR

LIVING WITH OTHERS

—for Arlie

Yesterday, I discovered my wife
often climbs our stairs on all fours.

In my lonely beastliness,
I thought I was alone,
the only four-legged climber, the forger
of paths through thickets to Kilimanjaro's summit.

In celebration then, side by side,
we went up the stairs on all our fours,
and after a few steps
our self-consciousness slid from us
and I growled low in the throat
and bit with blunt teeth my mate's shoulder and
she laughed low
in her throat,
and rubbed her haunches on mine.

At the top of the stairs
we rose on our human feet
and it was fine and fitting somehow;
it was Adam and Eve rising
out of themselves before the Fall—
or after; it was survivors on a raft
mad-eyed with joy
rising to the hum of a distant rescue.

I live for such moments.

ROOTED AND WAVERING

The seed I planted
has sprung into a sunflower
taller than myself.

We stand in the morning light
facing each other.
I am between
the sun and the sunflower.

Already the large head
is home for bejeweled insects and mites
whose names I'll never learn.

A small breeze comes by
and the yellow head
nods a few times on its springy stalk.
Yes, yes it says.

The breeze pivots above the garden,
swirls away part of the morning.
No, no says the sunflower.

I am the sunflower, rooted
and wavering
through a long day's
affirmations and denials,
dragging the sun
by its gold chain behind me.

DREAM OF THE SPLIT MAN

A child-woman
with fine black hair on her arms
operates in your split chest.
Open-heart surgery.
For some reason, she inspires
total confidence.

She reaches in with both hands,
lifts your heart gently.
"Look behind," she whispers.
"There's a blocked vein,
the vein that leads to your right arm."

Immediately, your sword arm
goes numb.
Your trigger finger,
your writing hand, your
hiking thumb, your palm
with its diagram of what you've made
of your life,
your fingers that play
the piano's high notes
(and a woman's)
go numb.
The hand you shake with,
stifle yawns with,
serve with, comb
your hair with, shave,
pick, manipulate the world with,
stiffens by your side.

But it's all right, somehow.
All these years,
your left hand, modest
but sinister accompanist,
has seen itself in the mirror
grown stronger.
Even now, clenching
and unclenching, it is learning
the ways of a fist.

TWO CHILDHOOD MEMORIES

I remember my first gun
and my first tangerine.
My father said never
point a gun at a live thing.
I was five and it was my first
gun and besides it was a toy.
I was five and I knew that.
So, I pointed the gun
at my father, at my mother.
It was a big black gun
and it wobbled a lot.
When I pulled the trigger
it went "click,"
and I think my father died.
What I remember about the tangerine
is how easily the skin came off.

THE HOMECOMING

After years away from the city
you return and find your father
in a family album suddenly grown
younger, grown younger like the cops
in squad cars patrolling the streets,
licensed teenagers, the faint
figure-eight imprints of prophylactics
still in their bulky wallets.
He is younger than you now,
knows less than you, though he tries
to hide it with a cocked head
and arched eyebrows. Your mother
a virgin beside him with a virgin's
smile. You are in that smile
the way the sun is in a coffee bean
or a good cigar, waiting
for the magic to release you.
And you are in your father's house now,
years later, somehow still a child,
but strangely father to the man at last,
waiting for the magic to release you.

THE WALK AT DUSK

The hour of repose.
The steaks and potatoes, the chicken
noodle soups, the pizzas
and cold glasses of milks
quietly turning into my neighbors.

The quiet streets.
The Fords and Chevys, the Buicks
and v.w.'s nuzzling the curbs
and winding down—like the suddenly
abandoned toys of children.
They wind down.
The ping of metal cooling,
the winding down.

The retirement home.
The golden light spilling
out of the aquarium windows
of the retirement home.
A golden light for the golden years.
The retiring, the golden retiring.

UNSEASONABLE BIRTHS

You see them occasionally,
the flies hatched in a warm
pocket of winter, the dull ones.
They lack something,
as if they knew their lives were all wrong.
They lack the fine maneuvers,
the athletic dodges of their summer cousins.
They fly in slow, wide circles,
buzzing in puzzled surprise.
You can almost pick them out of the air
with your thumb and forefinger.
They come from the last eggs of summer,
the last desperate deposits in the bank of the future.
Here they are, then, tricked into existence
by the central heating in a January house.
And so they have no choice
but to rise on warm air currents
and circle the huge, warm lamps
that float beneath ceilings like benign suns;
and when the suns get too hot,
the flies end up against the clean glass
of windows, buzzing in sporadic anger now,
a universe of white snow
just beyond their insect sight.

THOSE WHO DISAPPEAR

—for Sigitas Skrinska, boyhood friend

Sigitas, a name like my own,
alien—a name to be mocked
by the Ians and Trevors, the Brians and Malcolms,
the Australian descendents
of English and Irish petty-thieves.
And they did mock us,
but you were tall and blond
and at the age of sixteen
could jump your own height.

You're the only genuine
Missing Person I know.
Of all the thousands who disappear
out of the middle of their lives—
never come back from work one day, never
return from an errand—you're
the only one whose absence
ever touched me.

At eighteen you went Outback
and we never heard from you again.

You left a hole in our lives, left
your mother trapped in the Never-Never
between hope and loss,
unable for years to give herself wholly
to one or the other.

There were rumors of Foul Play.
Even violence or murder
we would accept better
than this vanishing into thin air,

this disappearing without a trace
(the clichés appropriate for once).

Now, years later and from half-way round the world,
I can still see you dimly
through the window of my own
gradual disappearance,
performing some mundane ritual—
eating, washing your hands, perhaps
combing your thin blond hair—
in your middle-age now
but still able, somehow,
to leap your own height.

BEATING FATHER FINALLY

On guard, check,
checkmate.
The game concludes
like the last inevitable notes
of a Beethoven symphony.
Bishop, knight, and rook
have left father's king
nowhere to go.
He sits in the corner
trapped, humbled.

The board dissolves
leaving a kitchen table by a window,
noises of chairs squeaking,
and the snow outside
suddenly falling faster.

A MAN WITH HIS WIFE

A man with his wife
away does the alone things
without guilt; perhaps
he walks about the town
for hours or lies
in the sun all afternoon;
perhaps he releases
a few million sperm,
like lemmings, to the sea.

True, the man feels
lost some of the time
not knowing where
to put his hands, but
he finds his pockets finally
and the obedient world
jumps back into place.

At night, the man still sleeps
on his own side. Perhaps
he dreams he makes
love to his wife
who becomes pregnant
and has a child—all
in that same night, all
in the space of a lifetime.

FOUR A.M. ON A FARM

No cars have gone by for hours.
Our white cat wears the fog

easily. In the barn eggs grow
into chickens, chickens into eggs.

Everywhere green fields slowly turn
to milk. From five miles up

the sound of a jet floats down
softly . . . inside,

men from Tokyo
dream of the strange farms below.

For them it is noon. They sleep
against the quiet argument of their bodies.

In two hours they will land
in New York with the sun. For myself,

I wish them well. I will be
in bed soon. A box-elder bug

walks into the house through an entrance
that has nothing to do with me.

Seven hawks hang above the farm
like some immense, slowly turning mobile.
They glide silently as blood, the sun
warm in their wings.
Beneath them, the rooster, his eye
cocked heavenward,
struts around his hens.

TOWARDS THE END OF SUMMER

Late at night I look out the window
at the geese sleeping in the grass,
their heads thrust deep into their wing-pits.
They ask nothing of me.
They lie washed by rain
dreaming of tall grass and wide marshes,
the migrations of dim ancestors.

EARLY SPRING MORNING

I sit in the backyard,
my hand around a cup of coffee,
the morning with its hand
around my shoulder.

Above me in the pine tree,
the blackbirds don't know
it's Sunday; their knees bend
the wrong way.

I sit on my land-
lady's garden chair
by her wooden picnic table.

The morning is a waitress who
wipes the dew away.
"Scramble two, honey,
and I'll take
a side order of bliss."

Easier done than said.

To my left
the alley tries to shock
me with its shamefaced
garbage. Just down
the street I can hear
the turkey plant boasting:

"I change turkeys into T.V. dinners;
I employ a thousand townswomen."

As always, I am impressed.
But not overly so, for here

it is the miracle
of backyard, the lost
garden found, the rare
benediction of being

where you want to be.

I look down at my feet.
My toes have split
my slippers and are growing
into the ground.
There are leaves sprouting on my knuckles.

A blackbird lands on my nose
(now a branch), its emerald head
cocked expectantly.

Just before my eyes turn
to knots, they catch
the pale moon rising
like a spirit face
in the fathomless well
of my coffee cup.

THE PACIFIC SLIDES UP THE BEACHES OF THE WEST COAST

You can hear it in these treetops
sheltering a farmhouse
in the middle of Minnesota.

You can hear the whale-song
in the bellow of the cows beyond the corn
and the crickets in the grass.

The swallow-rays dive and pivot
on air currents
and swim smoothly about the barn.

You know that if you dig straight down
you'll find a bright twisted shell and
you only have to pull out the earth-plug
to hear the sea there too.

As you walk back into the house,
you finger the side of your neck
searching for gill-slits and you know
some day there'll be a larger tide
than usual and things will
get back to normal.

GROWINGS

Remembering my father's hands
and the way they played
with moist earth
I too tried to raise vegetables.
From a garden patch
the size of a city
parking space
and with the help
of the municipality's water
I created twelve pea pods—or
fifty-two peas.

I ate those peas
one by one
as sadly as an ancient
chinaman
adding up the score
on his smooth abacus
and decided I was
not my father.

AT THE MOVIES IN A SMALL TOWN

I sit down inside,
absolutely alone—
sloping concrete floor;
smudged screen, as if
by huge thumb-prints;
the seat hard as a school desk.
I feel anxious
like a child kept after class.

Somewhere near the front row
a cricket plays his leg.

I realize suddenly
I can laugh or cry with total abandon—
what an opportunity!

I wish I could sit
in all two hundred seats at once.

II. CHARM

A MAN AND HIS LIFE

At night a man asleep turns to his life.
He tries to embrace it.
As always, it skips just out of his reach
and laughs at him.
He chases it frantically, his feet
heavy as unexploded bombs.
Effortlessly, his life dances before him.
He wants to grab it, to run
it through some complicated steps—
a tango, a fox-trot, perhaps a mazurka.
He wants to love his life,
but it will have nothing of that
and only giggles at him, rolling
its hips at a safe distance.

THE WAY HE'D LIKE IT

Let me be the man who
walking among tall trees
is struck by lightning,
but is not killed;
who somersaults in a cloud
fizzing with burnt hair
and lands on his feet, shoes smoking,
and shakes his head saying,
"Jesus, that smarts!"

Let me be the man
hit by the last ash
of a dissolving meteorite.
Let it light on my head
like a benediction.

Let me be the man who walks
away from shipwrecks.

In a leveled city,
let me be the man found
17 days later under a former
insurance building sucking
air through the plumbing saying
"I never really thought of giving up."

From all disasters let me rise
wholly. On my face,
let me have beautiful dueling scars.

RESPITE

In the middle of February in Minnesota,
unaccountably, the Bahamas show up
making fools of the rich
who have flown winter seeking them.

Throughout the city
the unemployed sit on their porches
in deck-chairs like retired fat-cats
on a luxury liner.
Steam rises out of warped planks;
cars chase each other down
the street like dolphins.

No matter a blizzard up north
is quietly mustering his men.
Today the sun is for the poor.

Somewhere, the first insect shows up,
proud and penitent
like a prodigal son, home
too early for his inheritance.

TO A FRIEND WHO HAS BEEN AN AMBULANCE DRIVER, A FIREMAN, AND A MORTICIAN, AND WHO IS NOW A TEACHER AND A POET

—for Laurence Milbourn

You deliberately sought the accidents
of others: the cars overturned in ditches
along quiet Wyoming highways,
the houses in your small town
that suddenly bloomed into flame—
these things drew you irresistibly.

What most of us couldn't look at
you looked at—steadily?
What did you see in the broken
faces of strangers?

Later, you learned to fix these faces,
to return them to relatives
as they remembered them, reconstructed
from favorite photographs.
Those who died violently
looked calm in death, sometimes
even proud, as if they had
just graduated from high school.

Now you teach and write.
Sometimes, in the middle of a sentence,
one of your student's eyes will fall out.
You are the only one who notices.
You know how to deal with this,
how to record the precise texture of it,
how to finish your sentence
with just the slightest suggestion of a pause.

THE MYOPIC

is usually most comfortable with books.
He likes to climb around words,
up and down letters like a child
in a jungle-gym. He is familiar
with small things, and can tell you
if a spider has thumbs, and how many.

He wears glasses in his public
life to share in public visions, but
his real life is at home, at night, after
the wife and kids have gone to bed.
He folds his glasses away and draws
the world in around him like a shawl.

He will sit for hours, legs outstretched,
feet stuck in the fog around him,
and examine very closely the latest
detailed maps of the moon.
Outside, for all he knows, a caravan
of dinosaurs might be rolling on by.

UNEMPLOYMENT COMPENSATION

On a Wednesday afternoon in late summer
the unemployed man wakes from a nap
on the dining room floor
between the piano and dining room table.

He is surrounded by wooden legs.

He feels like the victim of a catastrophe,
coming 'round now
to the distantly concerned stares of strangers.

"Lie still, buddy.
We've called for help.
You'll make it."

At such a moment
it is permitted for a man without a job
and with no prospects
to see his life clearly
in the underside of a wooden table,
unfinished, and full of beautiful knots.

ONE MAN'S POISON

In the men's room in the basement
of the Saint Paul Public Library
a man hands me a pint of whiskey
and asks me to open
the son of a bitch it's on too tight.
I do and am embarrassed
that I can so easily:
my mother's jars, my wife's jars
are tougher than this.
By a perverse alchemy
this man's wrists have turned to milk.
He's an alcoholic he says
and knows he may die any day now
but adds proudly
I ain't hurting no one but myself.
He thanks me and offers me a drink
as I stand in front of the urinal
trying to piss. I, standing in front
of a urinal in the basement of the Saint Paul
Public Library, politely decline—somehow
not much in my life
has prepared me for this.
Upstairs, I don't check out any books.

PASTORALE FOR SPRING

The new grass, the new lambs
eating the grass, the new calves
butting heads under the slow gaze
of bull-fathers beyond wire fences,
the sparrows flying with pieces of straw
in their beaks, the seagulls a thousand
miles from salt water eating worms
turned up by the plow,
the earth itself. . . .

                      It is not enough.
I go into the house and put on
Beethoven's 6th symphony, the *Pastorale*.
I listen to violins and oboes,
former trees, pretending to be winds,
birds and brooks. I listen to drums,
the hides of animals, trying to be
thunder.

                   It all works, somehow:
the thunder, controllable—a living room
thunder, and yet the living room a world, too.
Outside, the earth is being lifted
by the music, it is rising
out of itself, trees wave their arms
like mad conductors, the sky is breaking
into applause.

TRAVELING INTO THE BODY
(A National Geographic television special)

Finally we grow tired of the world's body,
the countless tribes, the alien
rituals of the dwellers of Katmandu
recorded by Somebody Somebody, Ph.D.,
the fertility dances frozen on impossible Ektachromes.

We return to the source of all journeys,
all documentaries: our own bodies,
our own illusive selves.
With the help of a technology
that coils all the way back to Adam and Eve,
we roll our eyes inward.

We float behind the eye of a camera,
wavering like a kiss, toward
the face of a human being.
We enter through parted lips, past
the gate of the teeth, through
the cavern of the mouth.

We gasp as the camera slips down the gullet
like a bucket down a well.
Suddenly we're where we've never been before
and it has the strange familiarity
of a dream. We're the snake
swallowing its own tail;
we're playing the old game
of hide-and-seek with the self.

We move through the close,
illuminated tunnel of a bronchial tube.
The camera seems to jiggle a little,
as if the cameraman were drunk with his discovery.
And who can blame him?

We are on the edge of claustrophobia,
but the director, a wise man with a sense of humor,
has provided a symphony to take along.
The music swells and keeps us brave
as the tube narrows.

Every few paces (or so it seems)
there is a fork—two dark holes.
(Two tubes diverged in a lung.)
We take the left, then the right
and then the right again.
The choices mount upon each other.
We feel cramped and suffocated as we draw
nearer to where air becomes blood.

A jump-cut: we are outside the body now
outside ourselves again,
looking at the lungs through an x-ray.
The film is speeded up;
the thousands of small branches of the bronchial tree
wave back and forth as if in a wind.
Look, it is the Burning Bush!
Behind it squats a plump Buddha
pulsing, pulsing, pulsing.

HOW TO READ A POEM

Come at it
the way you would
a pile of clothes on an empty beach at dawn.
Circle it slowly.
Hold the pieces up one by one.
Be a cop; ask questions.

If there are pockets, go through them.
The owner won't notice.
He is probably dead.
Are there any jewels? Fake? Real?
If there are footprints in the sand, where
do they lead? If to water,
don't jump to conclusions.
Have your men walk both ways
down the beach to check
for prints leading out.

Is there underwear?
A pile of clothes on a beach
with no underwear is immediately suspect.
It could well be an inauthentic pile.

If there is underwear
examine it closely. Be neither
embarrassed nor disgusted
by the stains. If you find
a pair of jockeys and a brassiere,
be on guard, be suspicious.
It could be a false lead. Remember
there is more here than meets the eye.

Pay close attention to labels,
but draw your conclusions
shrewdly, tentatively. Be on the lookout
for patterns and combinations
out of the ordinary: Robert Hall
and Florsheim, pleated trousers
and cowboy boots, neckties and baseball caps.
These all point to a mind capable of great whimsey.

Always remember your basic assumption:
You can tell a man from the clothes he wears,
but only while he wears them.
While you are examining his clothes,
the owner may be riding in
on the crest of a wave
twenty miles down the coast, smiling
and mouthing the sound of his new name.

COMPOST

The foods decay, the foods decay.
                                        Beneath
the roof of snow in dirt rooms the worms work,
mixing molecules, firing the slow burn,
the silent oven kindled against the teeth
of Winter gnawing above.
                              Below, weavers
shuttle and loom organic fabrics like words
woven in crossword puzzles.
                              The secret churning
goes on unseen as the cold wind sweeps
the cold land clean.
                    In Winter's womb
Spring grows in an architecture of breakings:
As the cellar crumbles the house grows; the rooms
burst above ground into flowers waving
their heads in the new light.
                              Everywhere tombs
explode and the sweet sap climbs from the grave.

AN OLD MAN'S DESIRE

Tongue of mine,
night bird, fly
to the day's almost-women,
the saplings of womanhood,
the ones alone now, sleeping
barely in dreams.
Rest finally
in the warm nests
of your beginnings; leave me now
at my best,
speechless.

AN HISTORICAL FACT AND A MEMORABLE FANCY

When Kant was composing
his *Critique of Pure Reason*
he would look up from his manuscript
at the tower in the center of town.
He gazed so long the trees grew up
and obscured his vision.
He informed the city fathers of Königsberg
and they gladly chopped down the trees.
Thus he was able to finish his work.

Here in the country outside my window
the trees tower and wave their arms mockingly.
I work anyway, here a word, there a line.

Always when I awake in the morning
I run to the window to see if this is the day
my three hundred farmers have arrived,
morning chores all done, murmuring
quietly, axes on their shoulders.

THE SCAR

I touch your belly half asleep.
It is still there.
I dream: A railroad track
on a green field, workmen dismantling it,
tie by tie, loading the long rusted iron
onto trucks. It is hot, the men sweat.
Suddenly, grass pushes up through the gravel,
fast, like a speeded-up movie.
The workmen grow smaller, their clothes
slip off their bodies
and fall like shadows at their feet.
The sun turns green.
The naked children join hands
and run in a circle, grass
up to their hips.
They break the circle and begin to leapfrog,
one over the other, one over the other.
Where they have been,
the grass waves and closes.

DOODLES

We find them around
the leavings of telephone
conversations clinging
to addresses, appointments;

around the notes
of committee members,
judges; in the margins
of grocery lists and aborted

poems. They are always
on the edges, sliding
away like vitreous floaters
when we try to see

them clearly. For all their ubiquity,
they are humble and basic:
flowers, stars, stick-men,
uncomplicated by the rules of

perspective and modeling.
They leave the loud shout
of the third dimension to Art.

They are content to whisper.

A POLITICAL POEM

At the corner cafe
where I sometimes eat
I ordered a raw egg
broken into a cup
no toast no coffee.
I tossed that egg down
my throat like a cossack
taking vodka.
I did it for shock
value, for the value of the shock.
I did it for the waitress
for my mother for the sunny siders
and hard boilers the over easys.
I did it for those hopelessly
scrambled by America.

THE MAP OF THE HAND

What territory is this?
What rivers, what boundaries?
Whose bones beneath the ancient mounds?

Life, head, heart, fate—
the lines that hold us up,
that cradle us in the deep,
rocking wind of our lives.

I stare down at my own hand
like a man awake in a dream,
flying above the earth.

WAKING

You wake one morning
and find the world is strange —
"Nay, 'tis ten times strange."
Just like that.

You become obsessed
with the thingness of things,
the ecstasy of the possibility of things.
Furniture begins to glow,
to say nothing of the heads of your friends.

You've dreamed of basements,
of cellars beneath the basements,
tunnels beneath the cellars, and caves
at the ends of the tunnels
filled with white light so intense
it made you weep with joy.

In your life
surfaces keep slipping away.
You fall into the warm ocean of nothing
you can fully understand.
You are a drowning man
waving at the stars. Your lungs explode
into gills.

III. STRANGENESS

THE NEW PHYSICS

— for Fritjof Capra

And so, the closer he looks at things, the farther away they seem. At dinner, after a hard day at the universe, he finds himself slipping through his food. His own hands wave at him from beyond a mountain of peas. Stars and planets dance with molecules on his fingertips. After a hard day with the universe, he tumbles through himself, flies through the dream galaxies of his own heart. In the very presence of his family he feels he is descending through an infinite series of Chinese boxes.

This morning, when he entered the little broom-closet of the electron looking for quarks and neutrinos, it opened into an immense hall, the hall into a plain — the Steppes of Mother Russia! He could see men hauling barges up the river, chanting faintly for their daily bread.

It's not that he longs for the old Newtonian Days, although something of plain matter and simple gravity might be reassuring, something of the good old equal-but-opposite forces. And it's not that he hasn't learned to balance comfortably on the see-saw of paradox. It's what he sees in the eyes of his children — the infinite black holes, the ransomed light at the center.

A MEDICAL FACT

At the precise moment of death
the pupil of the eye
opens its widest.

The white lights in ceilings,
the moon, sun
stars, comets, nebulae,
the great band of the Milky Way —
all fall into the brain.

There are no lights
too bright for the dying.

BURNING THE RAT

I find him lying by the door,
legs outstretched as if he died in mid-leap.
I pick him up by the tail.
He feels loose, beyond the first stiffness of death.
His molecules have realized the futility of hanging on;
they know the party's over, it's time to head home.

Suddenly, I want to burn this rat.
I surprise myself at how much I want this.
I want to save him from the slow
decay, the fetid rearrangement
of his parts — or so I tell myself.
But mostly, I want to see him burn.

I drop him on the wire screen
that covers the forty-gallon drum
I use for burning garbage.
I light the fire.
I am strangely satisfied.
As I expected, his whiskers furl
into quick question marks and are gone;
his fur bubbles, then turns black and dry.

The tail, the long nightmare of a tail,
holds on longer than I thought.

Hours later, it is the only thing left,
a white length of ash
like the backbone of something prehistoric
seen from a great distance.

OPENING DAY. DEER HUNTING SEASON

The lead bullets
From the steel barrels
Attached to the wooden stocks
Of the rifles
Kicking against the shoulders
Of the hunters
Return

(Slightly diverted
By the buck's head)

To the mountain.

GETTING READY

I'm the racer poised,
tense in his blocks.
It's been this way for years.
The cramps in my hamstrings
are beyond belief;
my eyes fixed on the finish line
focus into tears;
the bridges of my hands tremble.
I'm waiting for the gun,
the starter's gun.
He has been lifting it into position
for ages; generations
of sparrows come and go,
lining up along his outstretched arm.

THE INSTANT REPLAY

We can have it again
and again — speeded up, slowed down, stopped
at the crucial point:
the knockout punch,
the rare triple play, the race-car
exploding against the wall,
the suicide stepping off the ledge.
We can play it again and again Sam
to our heart's horrible content.
We can even have it reversed:
the diver sucked feet first out of the water,
landing on the board perfectly dry.
At night we dream with the help
of camera techniques:
jump-cuts, fade-outs, slow-mo.
The same old dreams: the snake pits,
the flying over vast cities,
the appointment we have with someone
somewhere, but have yet to keep.

MIDNIGHT CAVE, TEXAS: THE EXPERIMENT

— for Michel Siffre

A man descends into a cave
long abandoned by bats. For six months
the electrodes and wires of science
bristle from his head.

In the dark chest of the earth,
a hundred feet beneath the seasons
and with no clock but
the wound timepiece of himself,

he seeks his own rhythms.
Above him colleagues monitor
his vital functions
and turn the lights on

and off at his request.
His dreams, of course, are his own,
part of the self's short-circuit,
not to be monitored by the surface crew.

After the 130th cycle
(there are no days), after waking
in panic in absolute darkness,
he writes, "When you find yourself

alone, isolated
in a world totally without time,
face-to-face with yourself, all
the masks that you hide behind —

those that preserve your own illusions,
those that protect them before others —
finally fall, sometimes brutally."
The man sits on a rock

in the circle of light
around his pale-blue tent
for a succession of eternities
swaying mindlessly. He daydreams

of the dense jungles of Guatemala,
the sunlight filtering
through wet leaves. His boyhood
fantasy of finding Mayan relics

somehow sustains him:
"I will go to Central America
and I will regain control of my soul."
On the floor of the cave

the dust of ancient bat guano
filters, particle by fine particle,
through itself.

WAXING THE CAR

Seeing yourself suddenly
in the convex, flying-away-world
of the polished
hubcap, your hand
the largest part of you,
you stretched behind it, diminished
like the past —
like History itself
moving this huge appendage
back and forth against itself
across the invisible, chrome present.

SAILING

After years by the ocean
a man finds he learns to sail
in the middle of the country,
on the surface of a small lake with a woman's name
in a small boat with one sail.

All summer he skims back and forth
across the open, blue eye of the midwest.
The wind comes in from the northeast
most days and the man learns
how to seem to go against it, learns
of the natural always crouched
in the shadow of the unnatural.

Sometimes the wind stops
and the man is becalmed —
just like the old traders who sat for days
in the doldrums on the thin skin of the ocean,
nursing their scurveys
and grumbling over short grog rations.

And the man learns a certain language:
he watches the luff, beats windward, comes
hard-about, finally gets
port and starboard straight.

All summer, between the soft, silt bottom
and the blue sheath of the sky, he glides
back and forth across the modest lake
with the woman's name.

And at night
he dreams of infinite flat surfaces,
of flying at incredible speed,
one hand on the tiller, one on the mainsheet, leaning
far out over the sparkling surface, the sail
a transparent membrane, the wind
with its silent howl, a force
moving him from his own heart.

I picked up some seaweed
and felt the despair
of its collapse on the sand,
the change in its being, how
it lacked feathers for its new life
in the air, how it shrank
from its sudden acquaintance with dust.

#43

I watch you comb your hair,
the part down the middle.

I grow small. I climb
onto your head and lie
down in the part.

Your hair becomes water,
the Pacific Ocean. I lie
on the invisible seam, the waves
rising under me, parting
and flowing off to America and Asia.
They fall on the ears of those places
like hair.

I am happy
lying on my back in my hair-ocean.

A NIGHTMARE CONCERNING PRIESTS

They whirl down the aisles;
the congregation applauds.
Frankly, I'm frightened.
From the pulpit the bishop
shows us his armpits.
They are hairless
like a female trapeze artist's.
When he speaks, his teeth
click like dice and white hosts
tumble from his mouth.
The people don't mind;
they count it a blessing.
From up on the cross,
high above the altar, Christ
calls to the multitude
for someone to please,
please scratch his nose.
Twelve nuns in the front row
gaze at him sweetly.
One polishes
a wedding band against her habit.

THE ZEN OF HOUSEWORK

I look over my own shoulder
down my arms
to where they disappear under water
into hands inside pink rubber gloves
moiling among dinner dishes.

My hands lift a wine glass,
holding it by the stem and under the bowl.
It breaks the surface
like a chalice
rising from a medieval lake.

Full of the grey wine
of domesticity, the glass floats
to the level of my eyes.
Behind it, through the window
above the sink, the sun, among
a ceremony of sparrows and bare branches,
is setting in Western America.

I can see thousands of droplets
of steam — each a tiny spectrum — rising
from my goblet of grey wine.
They sway, changing directions
constantly — like a school of playful fish,
or like the sheer curtain
on the window to another world.

Ah, grey sacrament of the mundane!

IT MAY BE SOMETHING LIKE THIS

Inside my head
a bird.
Inside the bird's head
an elephant.
Inside the head of the elephant
the vast Serengeti Plain stretches for miles.
Perhaps it is noon.
The heat vibrates the trees
and the worms dig a few inches deeper.
Around the world
the sun is always rising always setting.
Perhaps the distant stars
are white holes inside my head.

SEEING, TASTING

Sitting on the porch,
leaves falling aslant the frame
I have created,
I feel like that nameless tribe
deep in some walled jungle
who anthropologists found had never
discovered perspective,
who when finding some deep clearing
and the distant beast
on the other edge, see
it as a small animal close,
who see all large things far
as small things near.

At a time like this,
on the porch on a fine fall day, I see
the neighbor's house across the street
as a doll's house, my neighbors
intricate, wonderful dolls.
I taste the shape and texture
of that house with my tongue: the cracked
weather-board, the emptiness of open windows,
the sudden tickle of a flight of sparrows.

I can't stop there. I shove
my tongue down the street, over parked
cars — the lovely rust, the warm metal.
My tongue absorbs accidents at intersections;
no one is injured, only inconvenienced.
My tongue grows larger from the richness
of its experience. It covers a neighborhood,
it covers the entire city, it moves out

over the vast heartland.
I can taste the Salt of the Earth,
the ocean that used to be there.
Everywhere, I feel the little raised bumps
of barns and farmhouses,
their desperate braille messages.

ECZEMA: A LOVE POEM

My skin itches
and after a while of trying
to transcend the itch,
I scratch — the slow climb to ecstasy;
perhaps my skin will orgasm.

No one thing touches another.

If we eliminated the space
between our molecules,
we — each of us — would fit
in a thimble:
tiny buckets of ash.

One plane of skin
seems to rub another.
Out of the space between
something nothing is touching festers.

SLEEP POEM

In sleep we reach into our Selves
like hands taking food from ovens.
Our Selves eat our Selves to save our Selves.
In the great kitchen of the night
we are both bread and knife.

In the city of the great kitchen of the night
we are the huge trucks that enter
purposefully as sperm
bringing ripe apricots from California.

In the universe of the city of the great kitchen of the night
we are the light from the star a billion years
behind our eyelids.

From the universe of the city of the great kitchen of the night
we awake into the suburbs of morning.
All day our Selves run from our Selves.
Like circles, we are on our own edges.

RUNNING DOWN SUMMIT AVENUE IN SAINT PAUL
IN A HEAVY SNOWFALL

Fat flakes of snow explode in my eyes.
Zero visibility,
the airport or weather bureau would say.

The world is a block long
and I am running in that world
past the ghostly houses of the rich.

Traffic lights appear,
catching and releasing phantom traffic.
I violate a red light.

Above me, the trees make a cathedral.
The altar is miles away.

I could run forever.

THE BLESSING

Lying on my stomach
in the backyard, my eyes
leave *War and Peace*, skip away
from lives more beautifully broken
than mine, fall on a dewdrop
hung in the shade of a blade of grass in the summer sun.
An insect — a kind of caterpillar —
no larger than a comma approaches,
his body folding and unfolding.
Under my nose, all of Mother Russia
and the drama of an insect and a drop of water.
My insect enters the dewdrop —
simply walks into it,
for a few seconds a timeless bug in amber.
He comes out, glistening in the summer air.
The dewdrop remains as before,
pure and clear, a collector of light,
self-contained in its miraculous simplicity. . . .
As if in the old gypsy woman's tent,
after a few predictable clichés
about the future, after
you've paid her a handful of coins
and are rising to leave, she smiles
and passes her hand through the crystal ball.
Lying on my stomach in the grass,
I seem to be looking over my own shoulder,
watching myself watch myself
pass in and out of solid domes
of light, impossibly clear demi-worlds.

OUR CAT'S FASCINATION WITH WATER

I wake to his weight on my chest, his half-closed eyes saying it's time to get up, human. In the bathroom, I turn on the faucet in the tub for him, the way I have most mornings the last two years. He jumps in. The black flames of his eyes widen. Again, he can't believe it, can't believe the silver chord hanging from the silver faucet, can't believe he lives in a world that gives him the same, new gift each morning; can't believe it, so he has to touch it, and then can't believe his paw goes right through it, and has to touch it again and again; and I, looking at his lost eyes, the wet paw, the tail flicking on the white porcelain, my untouchable other self on the silver surface of the mirror, can't believe it either.

THE NEW LAND

And so, I come to the new land, dragging the baggage of the old land with me. I impose the old maps on the new places. The old vegetation springs newly named in the new land.

I have traveled a great distance and still my arrival is a dream. The old land is under everything — like the old landscapes found glowing faintly under the skins of forgotten portraits.

My life is becoming like the kneading of bread, an endless turning in on itself; the dailiness alone sustains me.

My life is like the transitions of the language: I find myself in the translucent streets of the new land, shouting in a voice no one seems to hear: however, moreover, nonetheless, furthermore, . . .

A MAN JOURNEYS TO THE CENTER OF HIMSELF

— for Russell Edson

A man begins the long countdown that will bring him to his center . . . 100 . . . 99 . . . 98 . . . He goes through the rainbow of colors, meditating on each and absorbing its special gift.

Now he is in an elevator going down to the bottom of things. The floors slip by and the lit numbers above the door blink one by one indicating the slipping by of the floors which in turn represent the subterranean levels of this man.

Soon the man arrives at "B" — the basement, where all the pipes are, where it's hot and humming. The doors slide open and the man steps out into a dim passageway. He can feel moss on the walls and from somewhere the sound of dripping . . .

Now he is on a spiral, stone staircase; some torches sputter on the wall.

And now he arrives at a large subterranean lake and he is diving in naked and swimming past fish who with their wide eyes only seem curious. On the bottom of the lake he finds the rusty iron ring that opens the trapdoor.

He climbs into the waiting arms of a tree and slithers down its soft bark and lands on a vast, still plain wrapped in its night. The man pauses to reconnoiter . . . Ah yes, he remembers now.

He goes to the rim of the well and peers over the edge. Under the water's black surface floats the man's North Star looking like a common silver coin of the realm.

He looks up. Yes, there is the North Star's North Star! Suddenly he is confused; why is he here? Ah, the journey to the center of himself, he says. He focuses on the bottomless star and begins the long countdown . . .